D0603034

Art Center College Library
1700 Lida St.
Pasadena, CA 91103

721.0448
T866
2005

Art Center College Library
1700 Lida St.
Pasadena, CA 91103

The New WOOD House

The New
WOOD
House

JAMES GRAYSON TRULOVE

Bulfinch Press
New York • Boston

Copyright © 2005 by Grayson Publishing

All rights reserved. No part of this book may be reproduced in any form or by any electronic or mechanical means, including information storage and retrieval systems, without permission in writing from the publisher, except by a reviewer who may quote brief passages in a review.

Bulfinch Press

Time Warner Book Group
1271 Avenue of the Americas, New York, NY 10020
Visit our Web site at www.bulfinchpress.com

First Edition: September 2005

Library of Congress Cataloging-in-Publication Data

Trulove, James Grayson.
   The new wood house / James Grayson Trulove. — 1st ed.
      p. cm.
   ISBN 0-8212-6201-7
1. Building, Wooden — United States. 2. Architect-designed houses —
United States. 3. Architecture — United States — 20th century.
4. Architecture — United States — 21st century. I. Title.

NA7173.T78 2005
728 — dc22   2004024640

Full title page: Fallen Leaves, Maryann Thompson Architects;
photograph by Chuck Choi

PRINTED IN CHINA

Contents

Art Center College Library
1700 Lida St.
Pasadena, CA 91103

INTRODUCTION

More than any other building material, wood makes an undeniable impact on our senses. Walk into a house finished with wooden walls, floors, ceilings, and cabinets, and inhale deeply, then rejoice in the comforting scent of the wood. As you survey the room, marvel at the colors and patterns of the wood; it is difficult to resist the impulse to touch it, to feel its texture. Maryann Thompson, a Boston architect whose work is represented in this book (Geothermal House and Fallen Leaves), puts it this way: "Human beings are able to develop a meaningful relationship with wood because of our ability to have a heightened sensual experience of it." Acknowledging its place in the natural world, we are comforted by its presence in our homes and are in awe of its beauty.

Increasingly, we are also aware of the tenuous position wood holds on our planet, as vast tracts of trees are destroyed, not only for use in construction but to make way for more houses, roads, offices, and malls. Many architects and their clients, like those featured in this book, are working hard to reduce this impact on our forests by using only sustainably harvested timber and reclaimed lumber, often first used generations ago. It is in this reclaimed lumber that the emotional attachment to wood is at its strongest. Owners take pride in pointing to a floor that once functioned as a basketball court or to ceiling beams that formerly supported the roof of an abandoned factory and now serve a new master in a new venue.

Protection of existing trees on the site where a house is built can be of compelling importance, extending the emotional attachment of the material itself to the land that produces and sustains it. Most of the projects that follow are in rural or semirural locations surrounded by dense vegetation, often with stunning views of wetlands, an ocean, a lake, or forests. Protecting these sites even as they were subjected to man-made intervention required a special sensitivity and strong motivation on the part of the architects, the builders, and the clients.

In the early 1960s, the celebrated landscape architect Lawrence Halprin created a master plan for the Sea Ranch, a 5,000-acre residential community one hundred miles north of San Francisco on the California coast. He coined the phrase "living lightly on the land," which has become the guiding principle for the design and construction of the many hundreds of homes that have been built on this spectacular site, including Compass Rose (page 64) by Obie Bowman, the architect of many houses at the Sea Ranch. As with Compass Rose, all of the houses at the Sea Ranch are wood — usually redwood — and are allowed to weather to soft silver gray and settle quietly into the salt-sprayed landscape. So compelling is this idea of "living lightly on the land" that many architects have incorporated it into their practices; it is the rationale behind a large number of the designs in this book.

Finally, blurring the distinction between the interior and the exterior and making the house at one with the site is a design goal that was actively pursued by the architects of each of the houses that follow. When a wooden house is merged with the living, natural environment, the emotional bond with the material and its source comes full circle.

In Compass Rose, architect Obie Bowman uses the emotion of wood to transform the study. The house is carefully positioned on the site; here a view of the ocean is framed among the books as if it were a painting.
Photograph by Tom Rider

On the ocean side, two outdoor rooms bracket and
protect an open deck with stairs down to the beach.
The stairs serve to visually connect the elevated house
to the land. The original Wurster house at this location
was sited at grade, wind-shielded among the dunes.

STINSON BEACH HOME

A REINTERPRETATION

The design of this beach house was inspired by a William Wurster house that burned down on the site. Wurster is highly regarded for the simple, understated modern homes that he designed in the San Francisco Bay area in the mid-twentieth century. The architects sought to capture the spirit of the original house while meeting all current code requirements for houses in this high-risk coastal zone.

The new house's butterfly roofs frame views of both the Pacific Ocean and the Marin hills. The floor plan was shaped to create wind-protected pockets that can take advantage of the sun. On the ocean side, two outdoor rooms on opposite ends of the house accommodate dining and lounging. Sheltered by these corner rooms, the front deck leads down to the beach with broad steps.

Inside, the living room extends through the center of the house, enjoying light and views of the ocean and inland. The kitchen opens onto another sheltered deck with an outdoor fireplace for barbecuing. A large sink-level window in the kitchen features a view of the hills. The master bedroom faces the ocean.

Cedar siding was used for the exterior walls and recycled polymer for the decking. Inside, resawn Douglas fir siding lines the walls, and fir beams and decking are used for the ceiling. A lightweight sand-colored concrete floor runs through the house. The floor is raised with breakaway walls to accommodate any coastal flooding.

ARCHITECT
Turnbull Griffin & Haesloop Architects
PHOTOGRAPHERS
Procter Jones Jr.
Matthew Millman

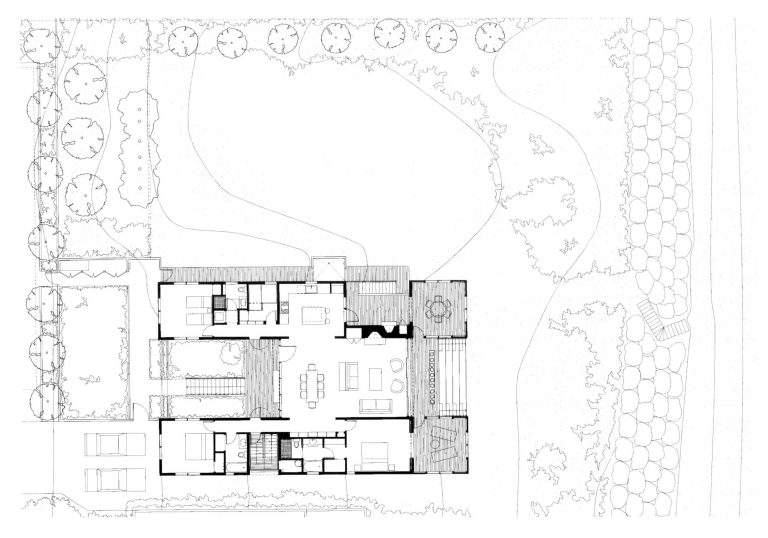

ELEVATION

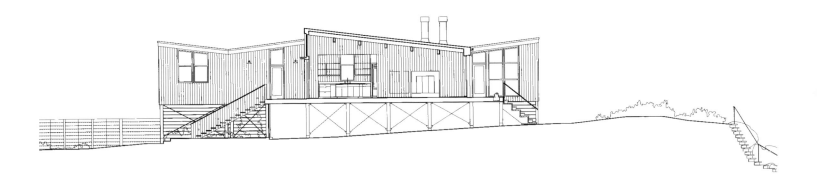

Sheltered decks off the living room and the kitchen
provide protection from the wind, making them suitable
for year-round entertaining.

*To meet current building codes along the ocean, the house
was raised and features breakaway walls, allowing big waves
to flow under the structure in a storm. From the oceanfront
deck, the Douglas fir interior gives off a soft, welcoming glow.*

*The living room, kitchen, and dining room embrace
the modernist spirit of the original house that occupied
this site for several decades.*

The landscape design by Nelson Byrd Landscape Architects
was driven by the clients' desire to live connected to the land
around them. The tightly woven plan incorporates a lap pool,
walking and hiking trails, and an entrance drive and court,
as well as areas for outdoor sculpture.

CHARLOTTE RESIDENCE

A GALLERY AND A HOME

This timber-framed house, with its gently arcing canopy enclosing a glass-and-steel pavilion, was designed for clients who are avid art collectors. The home functions as a gallery for works in a mixture of media, yet it is comfortably scaled for two people. Embedded in a gentle knoll on a wooded five-acre lot in central Virginia, the building is intimately connected to the landscape. A pair of perpendicular fieldstone walls flows through the house, creating a strong physical link between the home's interior and exterior.

The design emphasizes principles of sustainability through the use of natural materials and careful site orientation to maximize efficient use of energy. A wide variety of certified lumber was used, including Douglas fir glu-lam timbers and trim, beech flooring and cabinetry, teak and mahogany paneling, and spruce framing timber. Reclaimed white cedar siding was used for the exterior. The high-efficiency mechanical system relies on a ground-source loop to provide radiant heating and cooling through the lower level's floor slabs, significantly reducing energy costs. Forced-air heating and cooling are used on the upper floor.

A vaulted roof defines the primary living areas along the east-west axis to optimize solar exposure. Deep porches and large expanses of south-facing glazing frame panoramic views of the surrounding landscape while offering significant passive solar benefits, such as optimized interior day lighting, shade in summer, and low-angle light and heat in the winter. A two-story volume encloses the master bedroom and bath, guest rooms, and a private office behind the north-south fieldstone wall.

ARCHITECT
McDonough + Partners
PHOTOGRAPHER
Philip Beaurline

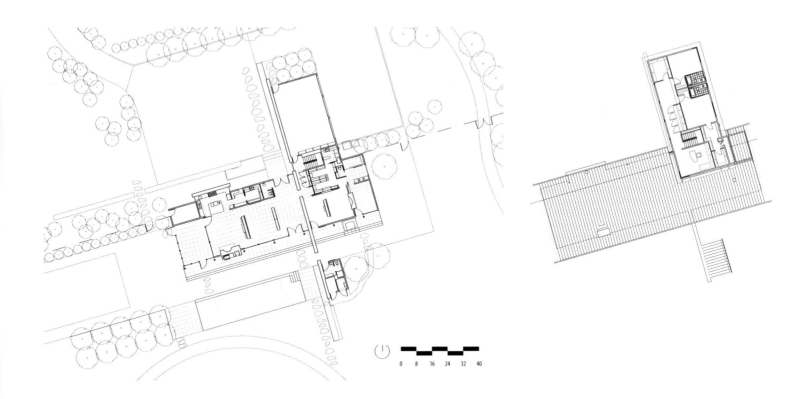

0 8 16 24 32 40

SECTION

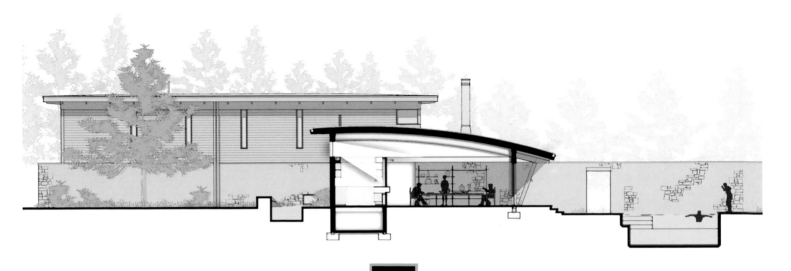

NORTH ELEVATION

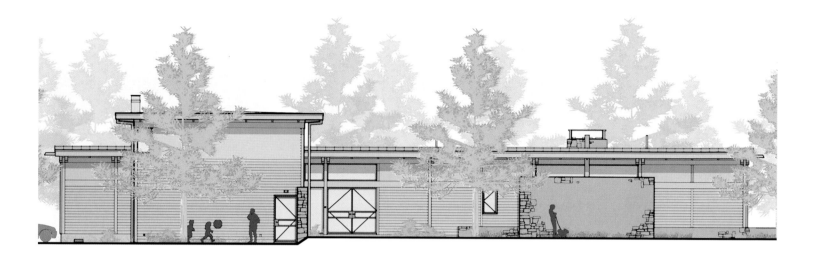

SITE PLAN

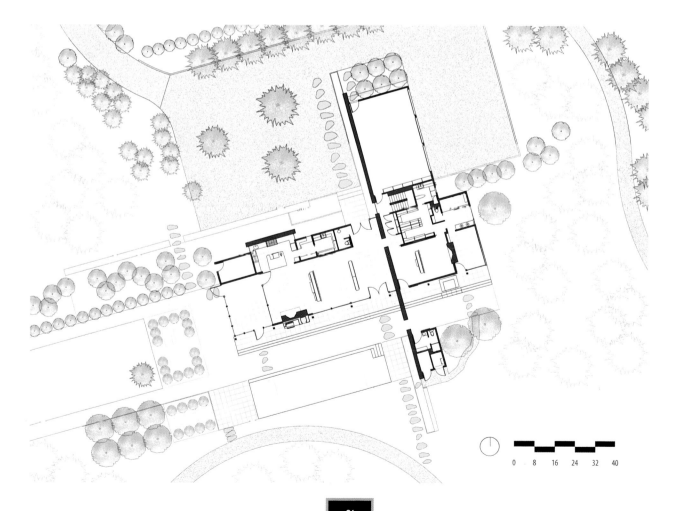

0   8   16   24   32   40

The use of natural materials like stone, plaster,
and a variety of woods reinforces the high level of craft
applied in building this home.

Custom-designed steel-framed beech cabinets in the public areas serve as room dividers, maximizing visual connections within these spaces.

The exterior doors and windows are steel sash.
Exterior porches and terraces use concrete pavers.
Texas limestone flooring accented with sea grass carpet
and ebonized beech, custom integrally colored plaster,
terrazzo, and local slate complete the materials palette.

The cabin is sited and designed to be connected to the
natural and man-made landscapes surrounding it.
The terne roof will turn a silvery gray over time,
as will the unstained cedar siding.

California Cabin

With a custom-built wood home, the site often has a strong impact on the final design. For this home in the mountainous regions of northern California, the influence of the site was of primary importance. The client, who had spent many years hiking and photographing the region, wanted a cabin that was tied to and celebrated the surrounding landscape. Reclaimed wood was used throughout the project, from the timber framing to the salvaged antique heart of pine flooring. The stone used for the fireplaces and foundation came from an abandoned quarry.

Granite, weathered cedar, and terne roofing enable the buildings — the main house, a garage, and a sauna — to sit comfortably in this stunning mountain location. Both interior and exterior detailing have been kept simple, allowing the beauty of the materials to dominate. Many of the objects and fixtures in the cabin were custom-made. Sinks were carved out of blocks of stone. Railings, light fixtures, and cabinet hardware were made by an artisan metalsmith. The design of the custom furniture was a collaboration between the furniture maker, the designer, and the client. The furniture was designed to be substantial and sturdy without referencing any particular style. All of the wood furniture was constructed from reclaimed 50-to-100-year-old white oak barn beams and rafters. In the living area, built-in cabinetry provides efficient storage and seating.

In this region, the building season lasts for only five months, so construction was undertaken over several summers. The remoteness of the site necessitated the use of solar panels and a backup generator for power.

ARCHITECT
Walker Warner Architects
PHOTOGRAPHER
Cesar Rubio

SECOND-FLOOR PLAN

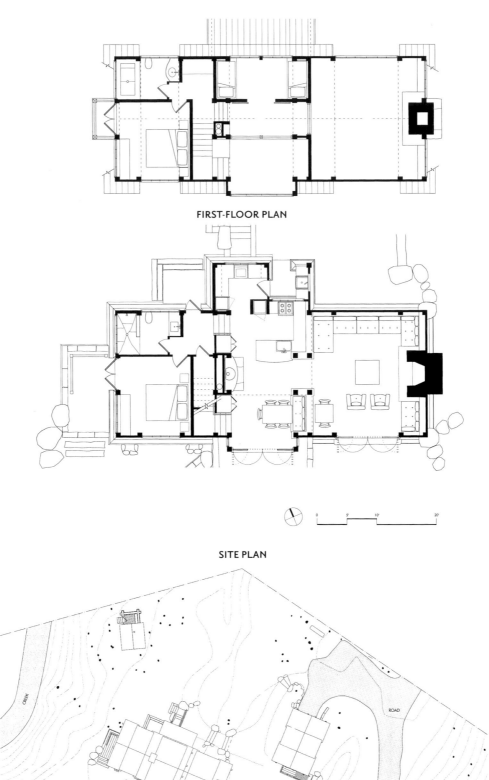

FIRST-FLOOR PLAN

SITE PLAN

SOUTH ELEVATION

NORTH ELEVATION

EAST ELEVATION   **WEST ELEVATION**

Single slabs of granite were used for the hearth and mantel. The only heat sources are the fireplace and a woodstove. Deep built-in benches line two walls of the living room to provide cozy seating and overflow sleeping space.

Art Center College of Design
Library
1700 Lida Street
Pasadena, Calif. 91103

The kitchen, dining room, and living room are all open
to one another, allowing them to share natural light and
views, and keeping each room compact and cozy.
The materials palette is simple and natural, keeping
the focus on the surrounding scenery.

The sinks in the master and guest bathrooms were carved out of an eight-inch-thick block of granite. Surfaces on the front and top of the sinks and on the backsplashes were left natural. The master bathtub was made from blocks of granite and has views of the granite mountain faces in the distance. Bedrooms are small, with drawers below a built-in bench and hooks on the wall providing the only clothing storage in the guest bedrooms.

Because the ceiling is extended to the outside,
the house appears to embrace the landscape.

GEOTHERMAL HOUSE

TRACKING THE SUN

This house consists of a series of horizontal planes that terrace along the edge of a south-facing hillside above a small pond in New England. Its design is based on the utopian modernist concept of blurring the distinction between inside and outside spaces. From the entry courtyard, the low profile of the house and the selective openings through the facade engage the visitor in a lively game of hide-and-reveal with the views that lie beyond.

The house is positioned on the site to take advantage of the daily path of the sun. The kitchen faces east, while the living room and its terrace face west for views of the setting sun. All of the rooms were designed to receive light on two sides, and the combined living, dining, and kitchen area receives light on four sides, thanks to the careful positioning of a clerestory. Outside the living room and master bedroom, large overhanging western red cedar trellises modulate the intense summer sun and admit the winter sun. Inside, the horizontal planes of the floor and the roof extend past the large openings of glass, visually connecting the interior and the exterior. All of the rooms enjoy cross ventilation, and geothermal technology provides both heating and air conditioning.

Western red cedar siding and Honduras mahogany were used on the exterior. Inside, the floors on the first level are reclaimed quarter-sawn white oak, and the second-level floors are Honduras mahogany.

ARCHITECT
Maryann Thompson Architects
PHOTOGRAPHER
Chuck Choi

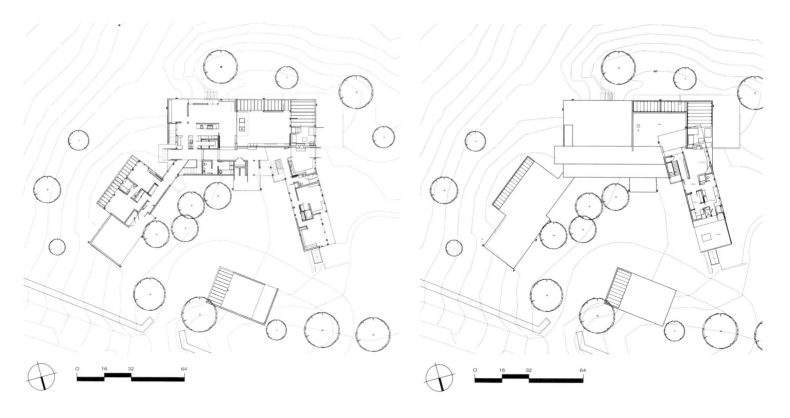

O   16   32   64

O   16   32   64

SITE PLAN

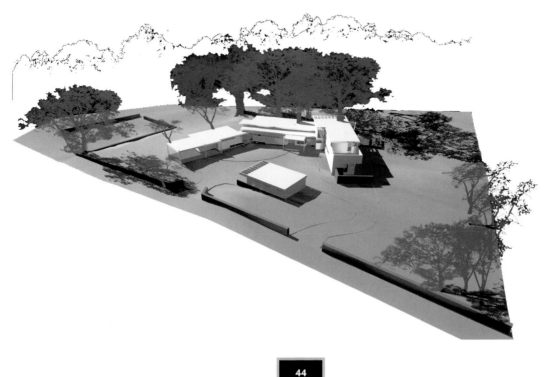

SOUTH ELEVATION

WEST ELEVATION

NORTH ELEVATION

Vertical western red cedar siding visually adds height to the house's horizontal planes, which terrace down the hillside.

Clerestory windows bring light from four sides into the
living and dining areas.

Inside, the materials palette is restrained, with Honduras
mahogany used for all trim and gray slate for the bathroom
tile and the fireplaces in the living-dining area and the master
bedroom. All major rooms have a view of the pond.

The living and dining rooms are on either side of the single-story portion of the house. The entire structure is wrapped in horizontally laid clear cedar planks.

BRADLEY-COHEN HOUSE

RECTANGULAR VOLUMES

The goal in designing this house was to create a large raised indoor-outdoor living space to take advantage of the broad views of the ocean that the building site afforded.

The house is composed of two rectangular volumes, each sheathed in clear cedar, valued for its consistent warm color and its suitability for use in this dry Southern California climate. The single-story portion of the house contains the living room, kitchen, and dining area, and is topped by a large viewing deck that is accessible from both interior and exterior stairs. A large Douglas fir trellis dominates the deck and provides protection from the sun.

The living space is an open plan, with exposed Douglas fir structural beams in the living and dining areas. Birch plywood paneling, used because it is easy to stain to match other woods, fills the space between the beams and was also used on the ceilings in the bedrooms. All cabinetry is made of cherrywood, chosen for its rich color and strength. Oversize French doors extend both the living and dining rooms out onto brick patios and the gardens at the front and rear of the house. Centrally located between the dining room and the living room is the kitchen. The entrance hallway that runs parallel to the living spaces extends through to the rear of the house and continues out to the garden, connecting the living spaces to the first-floor bedrooms. The adjacent two-story rectangular volume has three bedrooms on the ground floor and a master bedroom and office on the second.

ARCHITECT
Safdie Rabines Architects
PHOTOGRAPHER
Undine Pröhl

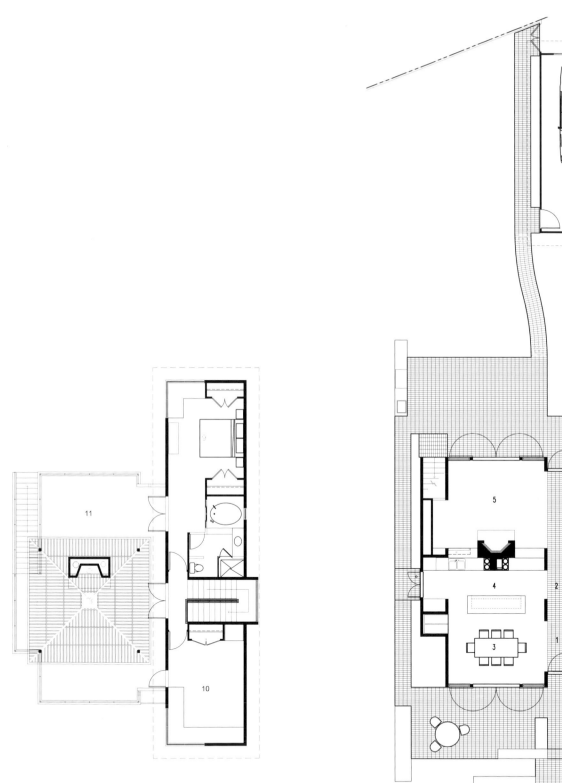

EAST ELEVATION

NORTH ELEVATION

WEST ELEVATION

SOUTH ELEVATION

A generous viewing deck is protected by a massive
Douglas fir trellis. It can be accessed from the
second-floor bedrooms or from outside stairs.
The Pacific Ocean is visible in the distance.

The living and dining rooms have exposed Douglas fir
structural beams. Between the beams is birch plywood.
Both rooms open up to terraces and gardens.

Art Center College of Design
Library
1700 Lida Street
Pasadena, Calif. 91103

The inspiration for this three-bedroom house with office,
library, two-car garage, darkroom, and courtyard was taken
from the wooden barns that are prevalent in this northern
California coastal region. The house is sited to provide
panoramic ocean views from its bluff-top location.

Compass Rose

Sited on a bluff-top lot overlooking the Pacific Ocean at the Sea Ranch in northern California, this 2,655-square-foot house bridges over the west side of a wind-protected courtyard to allow ocean views from the first-floor bedrooms and sitting room. A long corner solarium on the second floor captures views of the coast while extending the living, dining, and kitchen areas toward the ocean. Natural ventilation and cooling are provided through automated air intake vents and thermal exhaust chimneys.

In describing the design of this house, the architect notes that "much of my work is inspired by, and strives to empathize with, the characteristics of the site. Naturally weathered wood siding has a comfortable relationship with the natural landscape. Generations of barns, cabins, mine heads, and other structures have established a strong tradition of using weathered wood in the rural landscape." Heavy timber framing consisting of eight-inch-square redwood columns bolted to the foundation was used to construct the house, making it tight and secure in this windy, storm-prone location. The exterior is finished with redwood siding.

Inside, the timber framing is not hidden behind gypsum wallboard, but is a shared part of the space. The wall finishes, insulation, and waterproofing are all outside a wonderful array of wood columns, girts, haunches, beams, and knee braces holding the house secure to the land. All interior wood is Douglas fir, with a floor of red ash and exposed concrete on the grade.

ARCHITECT
Obie G. Bowman
PHOTOGRAPHER
Tom Rider

FLOOR PLAN   FRAMING ISOMETRIC

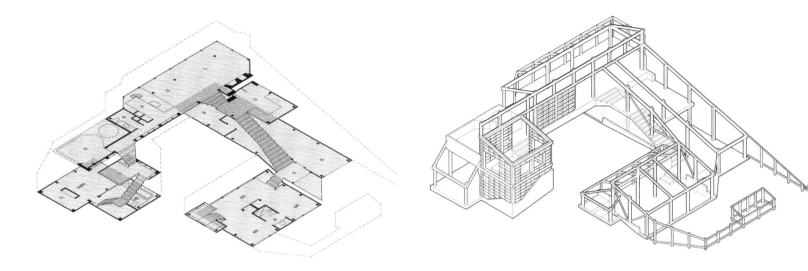

SITE PLAN

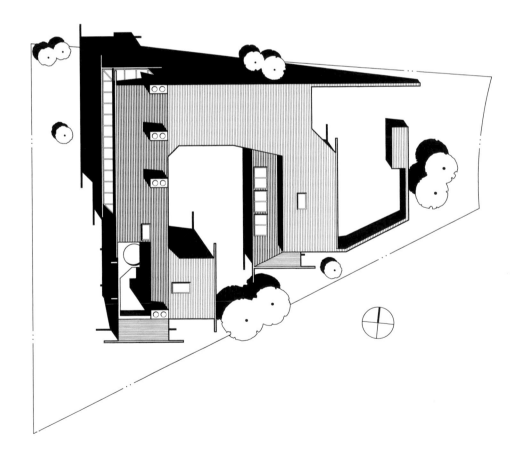

A long corner solarium captures views and sunlight while
extending the kitchen, dining, and living areas toward
the ocean. The rough-hewn redwood columns that
frame the house are visible throughout. Similarly, the
wood studding used to frame the wall of the office was
left exposed to provide shelving.

*All interior wood except the floors is Douglas fir. Its use
in the bedrooms, the stairway to the second-floor
solarium, and in other areas of the house creates a warm
and inviting atmosphere. Viewed from the exterior
at night, the house glows like a lantern.*

Since this house is occupied primarily during the summer
months, natural ventilation was a critical design concern.
The sloped ceiling of the main living space that faces the
water directs warm air to several sets of motorized awning
windows. These windows are shielded from rain and sun
by the overhanging roof.

ISLAND RESIDENCE

The site for this tightly programmed 2,000-square-foot home is a heavily wooded bluff overlooking Cape Cod Bay. The dwelling was designed to harmonize with and embrace the natural landscape of pine, bayberry, and oak trees. Sitting on a foundation that incorporates timbers and bluestone pavers, the home terraces up from the natural grade, appearing to blend into the hillside. The gray lead-coated copper fascia along the edge of the roof softens the transition between the house and the sky.

Clapboard siding, running trim, and corner boards are western red cedar. All exterior wood was finished with a clear stain to enhance the grain of the wood, allowing it to weather without turning gray. The cedar pergola above the second-floor deck and the angled roof brackets are detailed as paired members with single intermediate connections. Structurally the house is a combination of post-and-beam framing and conventional platform framing. Glu-lam beams and columns are exposed throughout the living and dining areas.

Bamboo flooring, a renewable resource, has been used extensively on the interior for its texture, color, and durability. Mahogany trim throughout the interior functions as a visual accent. The screened porch and the decks feature mahogany flooring, selected for its durability in the Cape Cod environment, where the salty atmosphere can be very destructive. The large custom cedar screens permit views and natural ventilation.

ARCHITECT
Hammer Architects
PHOTOGRAPHER
Eric Roth

SECOND-FLOOR PLAN

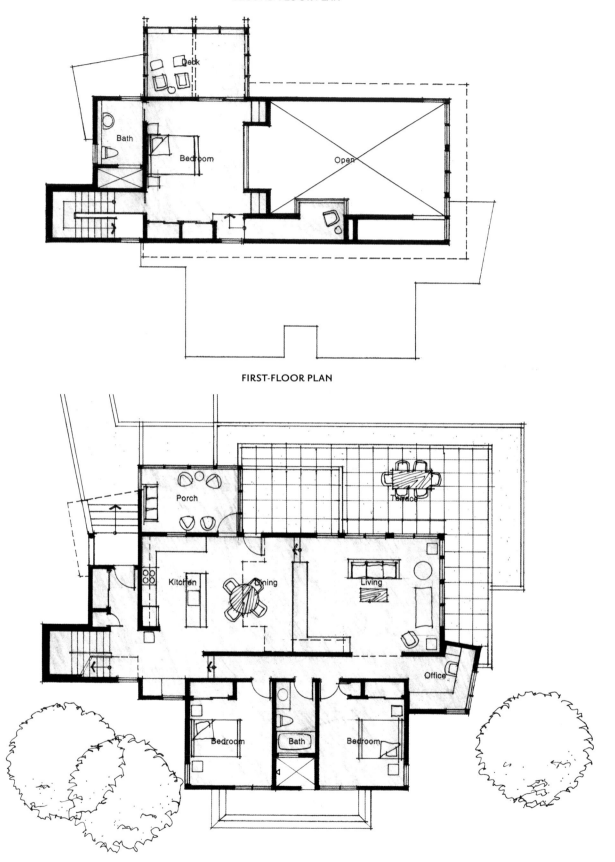

FIRST-FLOOR PLAN

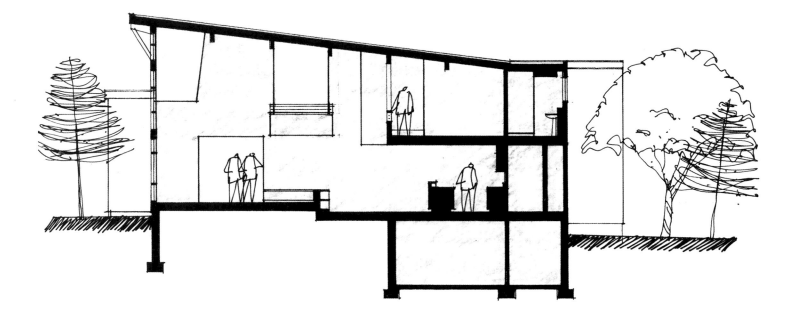

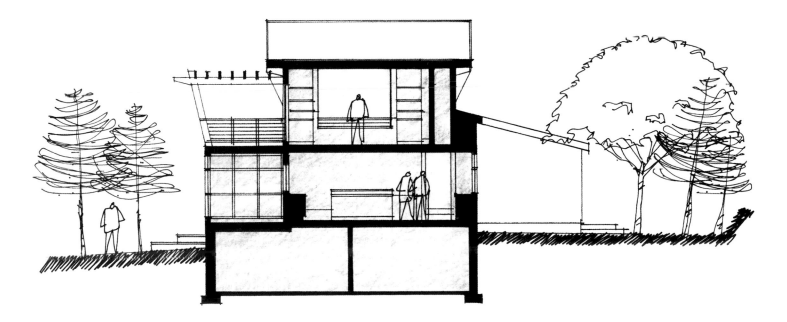

*A deck located above the screened porch is accessed from the
master bedroom. The pergola structure affords a shaded
outdoor retreat as an alternative to the open terrace.*

The two-story living-dining room faces north to the
primary view of Cape Cod Bay. The master bedroom
and a library-reading balcony open to the living room
from the second floor. Stainless steel cable railings
and mahogany trim adorn the stairway.

The plan of the house pivots around the central courtyard
on an axis defined by the main entry and the master
bedroom suite. Stepped decks made of sustainably
harvested danto wood surround the house. Oehme,
van Sweden designed the landscape.

PINE ISLAND RETREAT

SUSTAINABLE DESIGN STRATEGIES

Located on an eighty-five-acre island near the coast of South Carolina, this home is part of a "nature park" development surrounded by a private nature reserve and wildlife sanctuary. Community covenants encourage "simple designs" with regard to appropriate height, scale, and proportion, as well as attention to detail, the use of quality materials, and, most important, the application of sustainable strategies.

The design of this house recalls the state's "low-country" style, which evolved in the eighteenth century and featured architectural elements such as pitched roofs, raised pier foundations, deep overhangs, and large verandas, balconies, and porches.

The emphasis is on a rich yet simple palette of woods drawn largely from sustainably harvested sources. Reclaimed white oak timbers frame interior spaces that are trimmed and floored with clear-grade eastern white pine. Paneling was culled from blighted butternut trees in existing stands. Carpathian elm, burled maple, and laurel details further enrich the living spaces. With western red cedar siding and reclaimed western red cedar ceilings, beams, and window frames, the home's extremely durable exterior doesn't merely withstand the salt and spray of its marine setting, it weathers more beautifully with time. The "sinker" cypress columns that serve as the foundation were reclaimed from sources in Florida and the lower Mississippi. These columns provide a lustrous and responsible alternative to treated lumber.

ARCHITECT
McDonough + Partners
PHOTOGRAPHER
Richard Felber

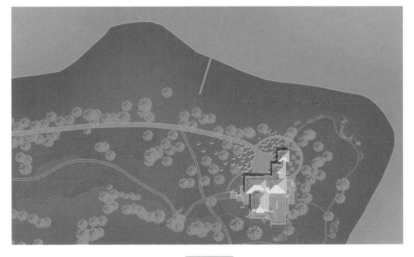

The decks tie the house into the landscape,
clearly defining entries and approaches while reducing
the effect of the foundation's eight-foot-high piers. Pathways
and outdoor "rooms" join the pavilions, framing views
of marshes, forests, and fields.

*Elements from the Japanese farmhouse tradition enrich
the low-country design elements, resulting in a series of
single-story pavilions that diminish the home's mass and
blur the boundaries between its interior and exterior.*

Currently used as a weekend and vacation home, the house
can easily transition to a primary home in the future due to
careful planning that included Internet access and other
amenities to facilitate telecommuting.

MAINE HOUSE

REFINED APPLICATION OF WOOD

Classic Maine camps were the inspiration for the design of this waterfront residence that will become a permanent home for a couple approaching retirement. At one with the natural landscape, porches, decks, bay windows, and alcoves offer a variety of vantage points for enjoying the lake, woodlands, and fields, as well as local fauna. From the stair landing (a favorite dog napping spot) to the painted tiles in the kitchen and the handpicked stones of the fireplace, the interior reflects the owners' interests and aesthetic judgments.

Simple sketches and models at the beginning of the design process helped the clients to get a sense of the character of the house and its spatial relationships. More detailed drawings defined specific spaces and illustrated how the house would be built. Many of the final details were a collaborative effort between the clients and the builder.

The owners' active engagement in the design process included sourcing building materials. Reclaimed barn timbers were used for the exposed frame. The Douglas fir floors and trim were locally milled. The fireplace keystone came from the lake, and the kitchen tiles were hand painted with images of loons and blue herons. An overheard comment by a passing canoeist confirmed the architect's and clients' success in creating a home with a genuine sense of place: "It looks like it has always been there."

ARCHITECT
John Cole
PHOTOGRAPHER
Brian Vanden Brink

SECTION

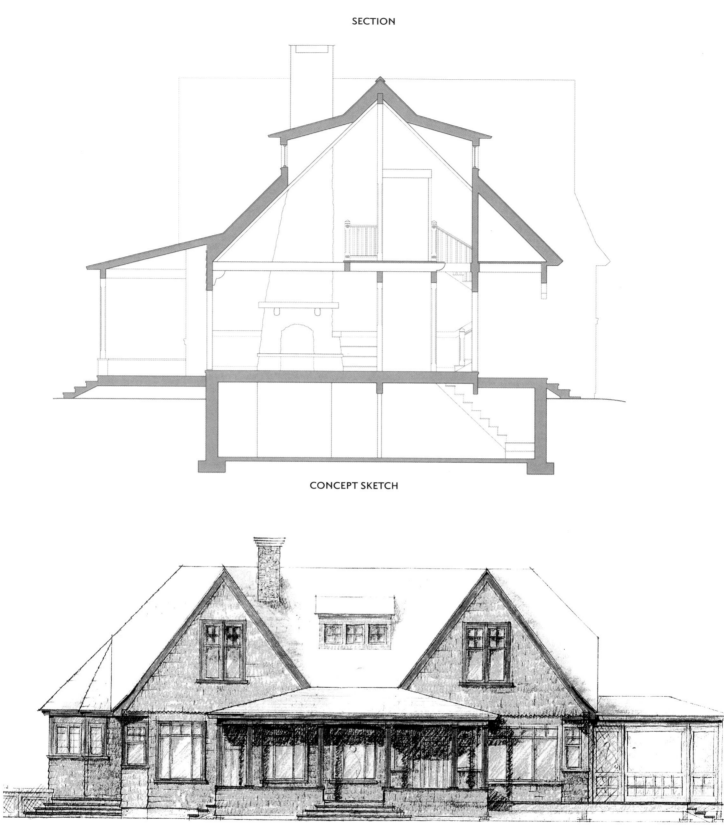

CONCEPT SKETCH

BARBER CAMP
11·10·00 WEST ELEV. ¼"=1'0"
J. COLE ARCHITECT

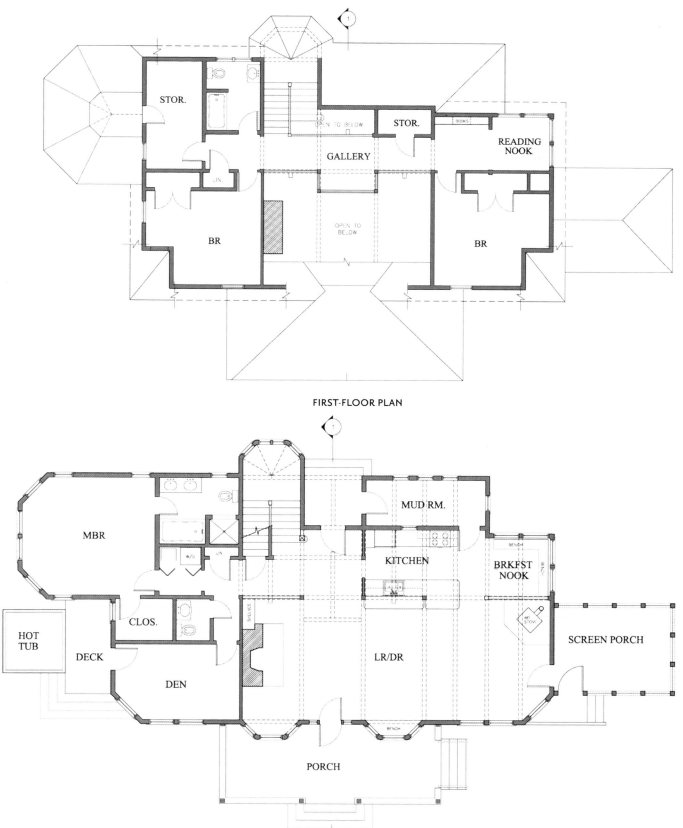

SECOND-FLOOR PLAN

STOR.

STOR.

GALLERY

READING NOOK

OPEN TO BELOW

BOOKS

LIN

BR

OPEN TO BELOW

BR

FIRST-FLOOR PLAN

MBR

MUD RM.

KITCHEN

BRKFST NOOK

W/D

LIN

CLOS.

HOT TUB

DECK

DEN

SHELVES

LR/DR

WD STOVE

SCREEN PORCH

BENCH

BENCH

PORCH

*Ample porches, decks, bay windows, and alcoves connect
this home closely with its natural surroundings.*

The exposed frame utilizes reclaimed barn
timbers. Locally milled Douglas fir flooring, ceilings, and
trim reference traditional
Maine camps. The fireplace keystone
came from the nearby lake.

*Sleeping quarters nest comfortably under the steeply pitched
roof. Rich in craft yet spare in design and detail,
this home has a sense of timelessness.*

A stone path leads from the street past the rectangular
block containing guest rooms, a studio, and the garage
to the entrance of the house.

SIMON HOUSE

CURVING ALONG THE OCEAN'S EDGE

This residence is located in a canyon, perched above the Pacific Ocean in Southern California, with dramatic views taking center stage. The house steps upward from the street toward the top of the canyon and is divided into two buildings connected by a glass vestibule. The public portion of the house, containing the living room, dining room, and kitchen, curves along the canyon's edge so that each room has an ocean view. The guest rooms, an art studio, and a garage are located in a rectangular block nearer the street. The house wraps around its site, forming an internal southern courtyard that is protected from ocean winds.

The entrance sequence, whether from the street or the garage, follows the slope of the site. From the street, a winding stone path climbs through wild grasses and cactuses, squeezes between the clear cedar wood wall of the front of the house and the curved plaster garden wall, and terminates at the front door. A gently stepping cedar and stone gallery leads to the entrance vestibule from the garage.

This vestibule links the different areas of the house, both inside and outside, offering the first glimpse of the canyon and the interior courtyard. Stone floors and cedar walls weave inside and outside the house, defining circulation. The ceiling in the main house curves upward toward the canyon, capturing the ocean views, and a low ceiling along the circulation spine provides space for clerestories, creating a more intimate scale.

Clear cedar was was chosen as the primary building material both inside and outside because of its warm, consistent color and for its durability in a semiarid climate like Southern California's.

ARCHITECT
Safdie Rabines Architects
PHOTOGRAPHER
Undine Pröhl

SECTIONS

ELEVATIONS

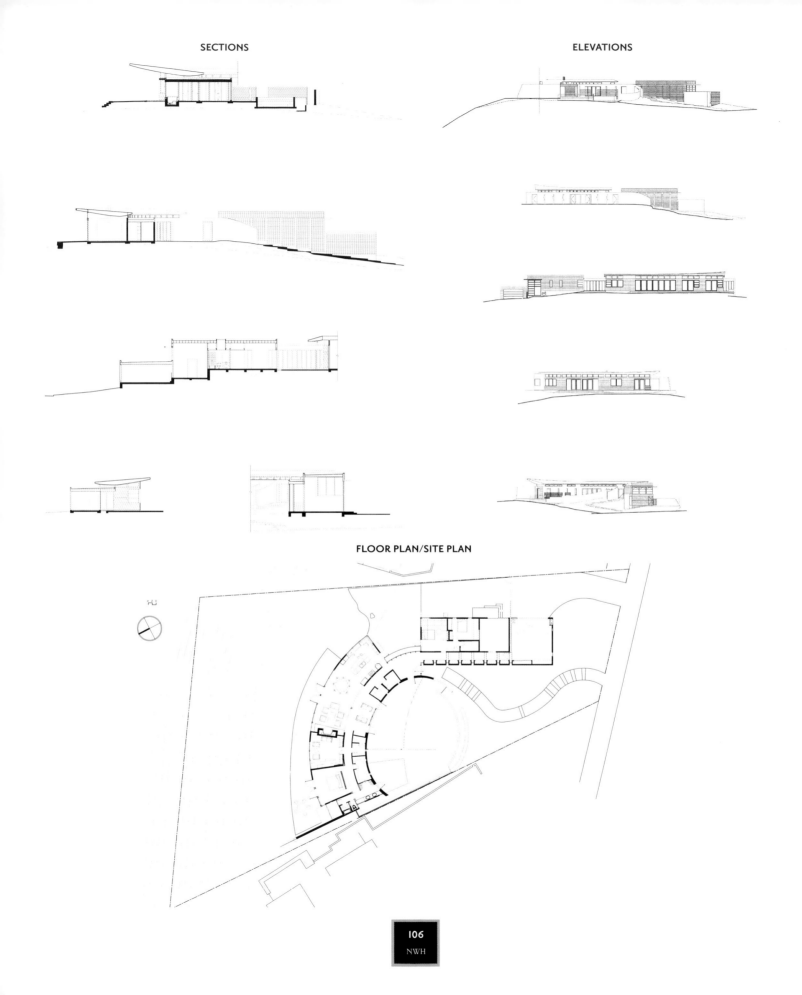

FLOOR PLAN/SITE PLAN

The house forms a landscaped central courtyard as it curves
along the edge of the canyon. A stucco wall continues
the curve of the house and encloses the courtyard,
protecting it from winds off the ocean.

The kitchen, living, and dining areas and the master bedroom enjoy sweeping views of the ocean as the house curves
along the edge of the canyon. The garage, studio, and guest
rooms are located away from the ocean, near the street.

*Narrow vertical windows along the west side of the
rectangular portion of the house admit bars of light into
the corridor connecting the garage to the entry vestibule.*

*The living and dining areas open to both the enclosed
courtyard and the ocean. A clerestory brings additional
southern light into the space. Cherrywood was used
for the cabinetry in the kitchen and master bath.
It was chosen for its strength, in a color to match
the warm tones of the cedar.*

*The sustainable qualities that are at the heart of this house
are immediately apparent at the entry, which is crowned
by a dramatic arch of recycled driftwood. The horizontal
siding on the exterior is reclaimed river cypress.*

Cove House

CONSERVING THE LAND

When a regional planning agency denied an application for a golf course on this large estate in Edgartown, Massachusetts, the Nature Conservancy purchased the property and looked for a suitable conservation-minded buyer to acquire it. An existing house was moved to a new location for moderate-income housing.

Sited at the east and west arms at the end of a cove, the new house is a low L-shaped horizontal design. Although it sits back from the water and remains visually unobtrusive from the cove, it nevertheless enjoys commanding views of the water and surrounding woodland. Landscaping consists of shrubs relocated from other parts of the property.

A host of salvaged and recycled material was used in construction, from reclaimed river cypress and yellow pine for interior and exterior woodwork to the massive driftwood arch that crowns the entry. The gnarly–oak tree shapes that support the second floor were harvested directly from the site. In order to keep the overall ecological impact of the dwelling small, it was decided to make the house a net energy producer. Exemplary energy efficiency was designed to be coupled with a wind turbine capable of satisfying all the home's energy needs.

ARCHITECT
South Mountain Company
PHOTOGRAPHER
Brian Vanden Brink

FLOOR PLAN

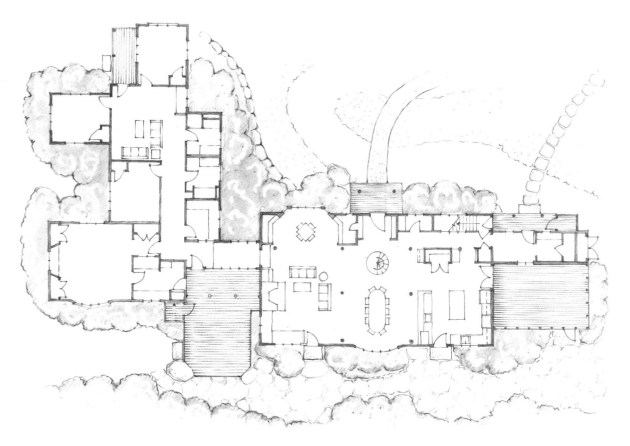

SITE PLAN

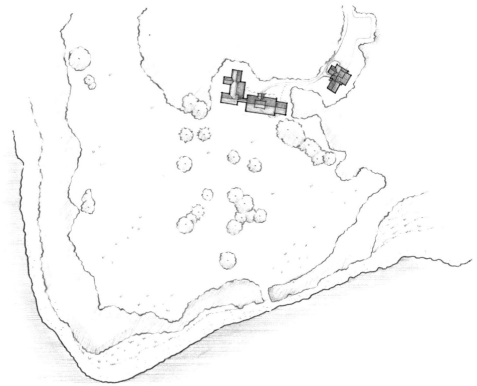

Looking back from the pond, the house sits low to the
ground. Its gray slate roof and graying cedar clapboard blend
quietly into the natural landscape. The front door is custom-
made from redwood beer tank staves and salvaged driftwood.

Oak tree limbs harvested from the property support
the second floor. Built-ins and custom interior doors
are made of salvaged cypress.

A driftwood mantel adorns the fieldstone fireplace.
The floors and trim throughout the house are salvaged pine,
as is the custom spiral staircase. The dining room
window presents a sweeping view of the cove.

Walking to the house, one comes to a bridge made of metal
grating. Looking through the grating presents an experience
of floating above the ground. The grating allows rainwater to
pass directly through the bridge. All of the surfaces that lead
to the house are made of this material. The entry door, which
pivots, is stained cedar trimmed with the Brazilian hardwood
epey. Horizontal cedar siding finishes the exterior.

VILLALUCY

FLOATING ABOVE THE LAND

Villalucy is a 1,400-square-foot house on a six-acre wooded site above the Strait of Juan de Fuca between Washington and British Columbia. A mandate to create a dwelling environmentally sensitive to this dramatic site influenced the design, materials selection, and methods of fabrication.

The house is supported by steel columns and beams that allow the structure to float above the ground and the lot to slope under the house, where rainwater from the roof is directed to irrigate the vegetation. The exterior is clad with a rain wall system made of horizontal cedar boards. The cedar is held away from the house by vertical battens so that all sides are exposed to the air and can dry out. This is particularly important in the Northwest, where sunshine can be rare. This construction technique also permits a thinner than normal stain to be used on the wood, letting the natural beauty of the grain dominate. Alder, a hardwood with even color, was used to frame the windows.

A building material called lite ply was used for the interior walls and ceiling surfaces instead of drywall. It is made of poplar and is considered a renewable product. Lite ply is distinguished by its even grain, bone white appearance, and light weight. The concrete floors contain radiant heat. Metal and glass complete the materials list for the interior.

ARCHITECT
WPA
PHOTOGRAPHER
Lara Swimmer

FLOOR PLAN

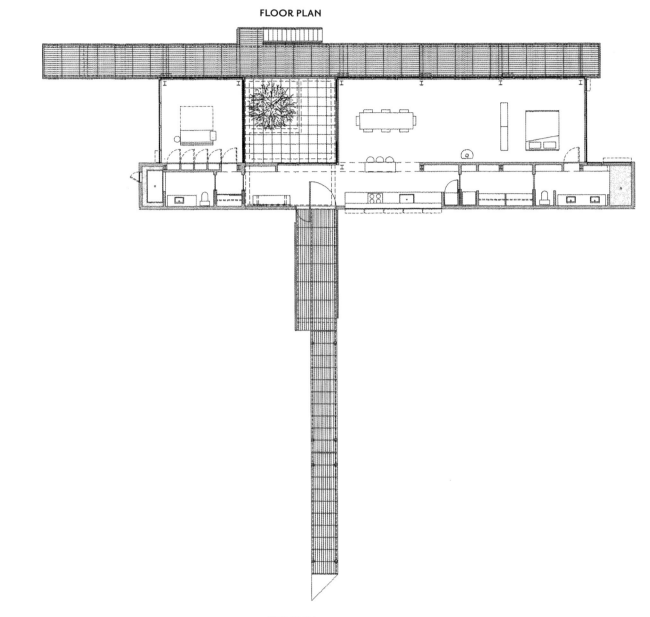

SITE PLAN

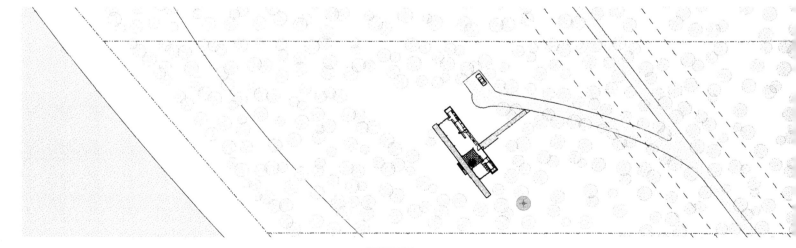

EAST ELEVATION

WEST ELEVATION

NORTH ELEVATION

SOUTH ELEVATION

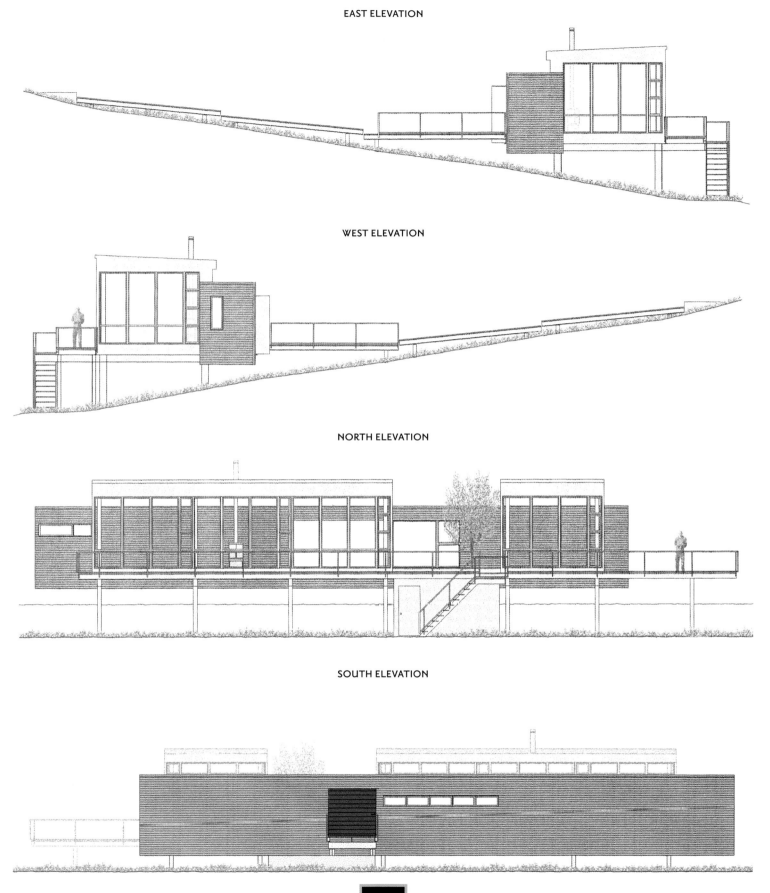

The house is organized into two parts. The opaque part
is referred to as the "bar" and the transparent part
is referred to as the "stage." The bar contains the kitchen,
bathrooms, laundry, storage, and dressing areas. It is long,
low, and narrow, with few windows. The stage is a large
open space separated by a courtyard. On one side are the
dining and living areas and master bedroom and on
the other side is the guest bedroom.

The exterior cedar cladding continues into the house,
unstained. The ceilings are covered with lite ply.
The eastern maple–top dining table was designed by
the architects. Poured concrete with embedded
radiant heating was used for the flooring.

The kitchen cabinets are birch plywood. The entry door,
to the right, is unstained on the interior side. The guest
bathroom walls and ceiling are covered with lite ply.
Surrounded by glass, the guest bedroom has views of
the water and the surrounding vegetation.

The lap pool visually links the garage to the main house.
The primary siding is 1-by-12-inch rough redwood boards;
the contrasting "lean-tos" are sheathed in corrugated
metal cladding.

WEBER RESIDENCE

FOLLOWING THE CONTOURS OF THE LAND

A man-made plateau atop a steeply sloping hill with expansive views across Sonoma County, California, is the setting for this armadillolike dwelling with a separate garage and guest quarters. Since this plateau was essentially the only usable space on the site, the house and garage are separated into two long, narrow wall-like structures that define a courtyard with a lap pool between them. At the garage, a portal provides access to this courtyard. The house also has a portal that provides access to the sloping ridge and separates the guest quarters from the main house.

Hip roofs on both the garage and the house make the structures appear to hug the hilltop. The unfinished vertical redwood siding will age a silver gray, matching the corrugated metal cladding used on the "lean-tos" and blending the house into the landscape. Redwood siding is more challenging to use inland than on the coast, according to the architect. The summer dryness reduces moisture content in the boards, resulting in faster and greater shrinking or swelling, depending on the severity of the season. Boards that have been dried to their final, stabilized moisture content will minimize this problem, as will thicker, vertical-grained boards. Applying a sealer reduces surface weathering and retards rapid changes in moisture content throughout the year, but these finishes require pigments to resist ultraviolet degradation and usually change the natural appearance of the wood. In addition, they must be reapplied every few years to remain effective.

ARCHITECT
Obie G. Bowman
PHOTOGRAPHER
Tom Rider

SECOND-FLOOR PLAN

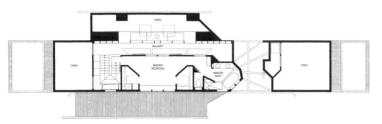

0 5 10 25

FIRST-FLOOR PLAN

0 5 10 25

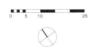

SITE PLAN

The house extends over the crest of the hill,
following its contours. An outdoor dining terrace
and barbecue are situated between the house and the
guest quarters. The garage portal is embellished
with an oversized redwood log gutter.

The living and dining areas open onto a long covered porch.
Inside, exposed Douglas fir beams and joists celebrate the
bones of the building. A piano alcove and a fireplace bracket
this space. The two-story kitchen ceiling is adorned with
skylights bathing the work area in natural light. Windows
are flush with the granite countertops. The stainless steel
kitchen hood comes complete with earthquake bracing.

Two stories of storage and display space were created
along the main axis of the house using exposed 2-by-10-inch
Douglas fir studs and blocking. Across from this wall
of storage is the fireplace alcove, which contains firewood
and television and audio equipment. The doors are
gun-blued steel with galvanized-steel trim.

Additional storage and display platforms are provided at
the stair to the master bedroom. At the guest quarters entry,
a window at the vanity sink overlooks the bedroom. In the
master bedroom, skylights and the kitchen ceiling are visible
through an exposed framing wall. Sliding barn doors beyond
the openings can close for privacy. The southern face
of the house is shaded from the sun with a covered porch
and second-floor sunshades.

Extensive terraces and a large screened porch accommodate
frequent entertaining. The pool house floats over a
constructed wetland.

VIRGINIA BEACH HOUSE

A NAUTICAL MOTIF

S ited along the shore of an ecologically sensitive cove on Lynnhaven Bay in Virginia, this house and the adjacent pool house enjoy extensive views of a constructed wetland pond and preserved specimen vegetation, including plantings of native species of trees, shrubs, and grasses that complement the cove's pines, black locusts, and white, red, and live oaks. In keeping with the nautical setting, the twin arched roofs of this residence hover sail-like above clerestory windows and wooden walls along the shoreline. It was designed as a primary residence for a family of six and is equipped with facilities for frequent entertaining.

The design makes extensive use of a variety of woods, and, thanks to the enthusiastic support of a local building materials supplier, the vast majority of lumber used was sustainably harvested or certified by the Forest Stewardship Council. Certified Spanish cedar shiplap siding was used on the exterior. Inside, two barrel-vault ceilings of tongue-and-groove cherry float above clerestory windows that admit abundant light. Over time, this light will deepen the rich tones of the cherry floors and millwork.

A central pavilion joins the house's north and south wings, clearly defining its public and private spaces. A grass-covered roof that doubles as an elevated patio covers the pavilion, which houses the kitchen and family room.

ARCHITECT
McDonough + Partners
PHOTOGRAPHER
Prakash Patel

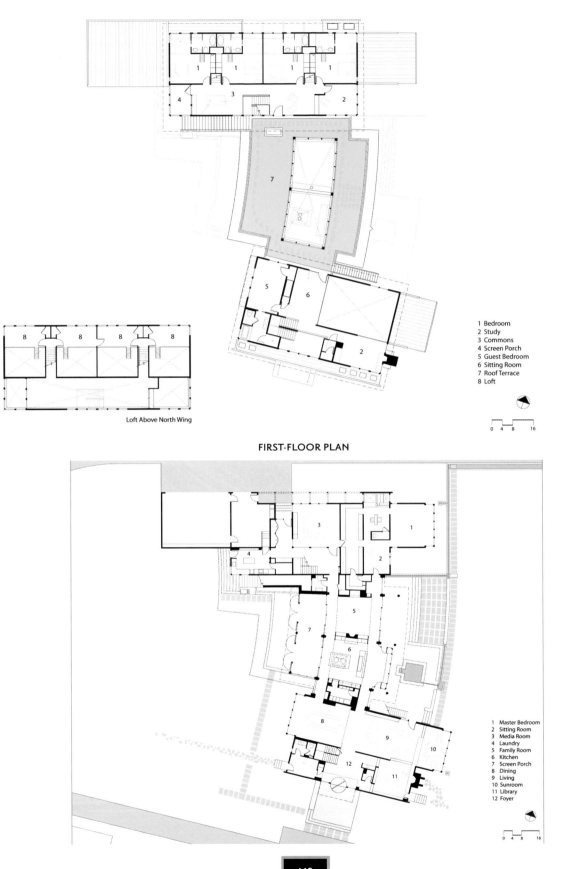

SECOND-FLOOR PLAN

Loft Above North Wing

1 Bedroom
2 Study
3 Commons
4 Screen Porch
5 Guest Bedroom
6 Sitting Room
7 Roof Terrace
8 Loft

0 4 8   16

FIRST-FLOOR PLAN

1 Master Bedroom
2 Sitting Room
3 Media Room
4 Laundry
5 Family Room
6 Kitchen
7 Screen Porch
8 Dining
9 Living
10 Sunroom
11 Library
12 Foyer

0 4 8   16

NORTH ELEVATION

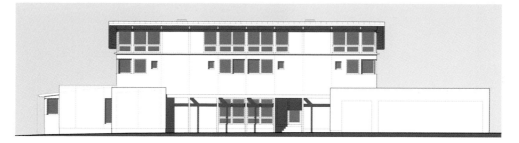

SOUTH ELEVATION

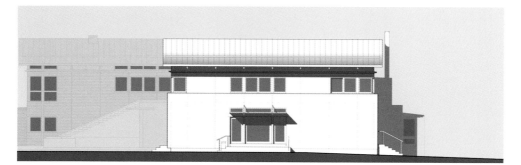

SECTION THRU CENTER WING

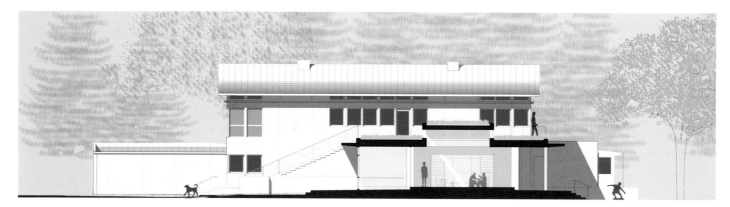

SECTION THRU NORTH AND SOUTH WINGS

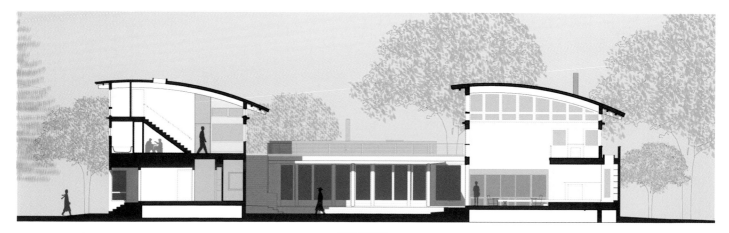

*The pavilion separating the two vaulted-roof wings
has a grass-covered roof that serves as a patio
for the upstairs bedrooms.*

*The numerous clerestory windows bathe the interior in
natural light. Much of the furniture, including the
dining tables, was designed by the architects.*

The pavilion contains the living room. Cherry was
used for all interior wood finishes and trim.
The extensive use of wood, both inside and out,
serves to integrate the modern lines and profile of the
house into the site, connecting it to the landscape.

The southern approach to the multilayered house is via a dirt entry drive that winds up the wooded slope. The house blocks the ocean view, first revealed inside from the elevated living room.

FALLEN LEAVES

LAYERS OF HORIZONTAL PLANES

This summerhouse is located on top of a broad and rolling hill on Martha's Vineyard. It is a windswept site with ocean views to the north and a heavily trafficked road to the south. The design challenge, therefore, was to determine how best to bring light in from the south elevation while blocking out the noise and view of the road. The house is conceived as a series of horizontal planes inspired by the layering of fallen leaves present on the site. These layers play gently against one another, admitting cracks and fissures of south-facing light. A sloping glass roof overlaps the north wall of the house, and large sliding doors open onto the deck and the ocean. To the south, large clerestory windows flood the upper-level public rooms with light.

The entry to the house was planned so that the ocean views would be hidden until the visitor has entered the elevated living room. Guest bedrooms are on the ground floor and they open directly onto the beach. Ships' prisms, like those found on the Vineyard's old schooners, are embedded in the floorboards of the upper-level deck and light the stone patio off the bedrooms below.

The exterior is sheathed in horizontal western red cedar, and Alaskan yellow cedar was used to trim the windows and doors. Alaskan yellow cedar shingles cover the roof. The exterior decks were constructed of Honduras mahogany. Bamboo strip flooring with a natural finish was used inside, where the stair treads and landing are clear maple.

ARCHITECT
Maryann Thompson Architects
PHOTOGRAPHER
Chuck Choi

FIRST-FLOOR PLAN

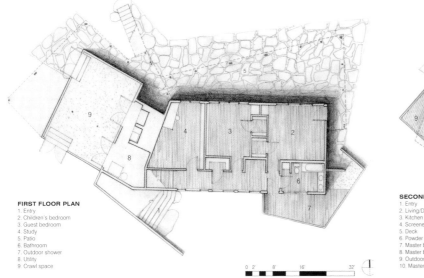

FIRST FLOOR PLAN
1. Entry
2. Children's bedroom
3. Guest bedroom
4. Study
5. Patio
6. Bathroom
7. Outdoor shower
8. Utility
9. Crawl space

0 2' 8' 16' 32'

SECOND-FLOOR PLAN

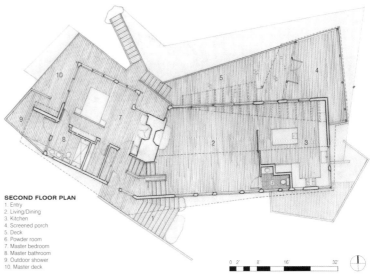

SECOND FLOOR PLAN
1. Entry
2. Living/Dining
3. Kitchen
4. Screened porch
5. Deck
6. Powder room
7. Master bedroom
8. Master bathroom
9. Outdoor shower
10. Master deck

0 2' 8' 16' 32'

SITE PLAN

EAST ELEVATION

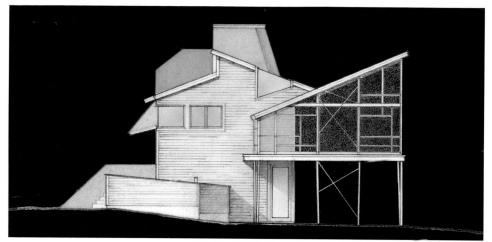

WEST ELEVATION

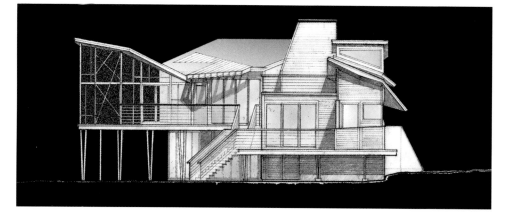

NORTH ELEVATION

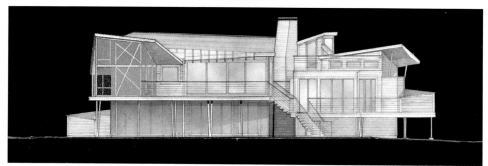

SOUTH ELEVATION

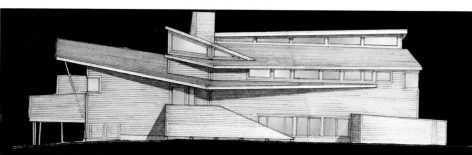

A wall restricts the view from the entry stairs.
Carefully placed clerestory windows admit southern light,
and the north side features the ocean views.

Guest bedrooms are located on the ground floor and
open directly outside. Large sliding doors open
onto the screened porch and deck.

A sloping glass roof over the living and dining areas brings
additional light into the house. The floors are
naturally finished bamboo.

The glass roof continues into the kitchen area, where the cabinets
are beech wood. Bathrooms are finished in slate and stone.
At 2,000 square feet, the house is modest in size but
grand in its dominance of the hilltop site.

Materials and Finishes

Stinson Beach Home

www.tgharchs.com

Exterior: Cedar siding, recycled polymer decking

Interior: Resawn Douglas fir siding, beams, and ceiling

Finishes

Exterior: No finishes used

Interior: No finishes used

Charlotte Residence

www.mcdonoughpartners.com

Exterior: FSC certified cypress siding, spruce framing timber

Interior: Douglas fir glu-lam timbers and trim, beech flooring and cabinetry, teak and mahogany panels

Finishes

Exterior: Weather Tec

Interior: Safecoat "Polyureseal" BP satin

California Cabin

www.walker-warner.com

Exterior: Reclaimed timber framing, weathered vertical cedar

Interior: Reclaimed Douglas fir barn beams, rafters, and paneling; antique heart of pine flooring

Finishes

Exterior: Benite sealer for Douglas fir, no finish for cedar siding

Interior: Livos Meldos Hard Oil finish

Geothermal House

www.maryannthompson.com

Exterior: Western red cedar vertical siding and trellis, western red cedar horizontal shiplap, Honduras mahogany trim

Interior: Quarter-sawn white oak floors and dining room wall; Honduras mahogany entry floor and walls, master bedroom suite floor; antique heart of pine bookcases, countertops

Finishes

Exterior: Stained

Interior: Clear sealer finishes

Bradley-Cohen House

www.safdierabines.com

Exterior: Clear cedar, Douglas fir trellis

Interior: Douglas fir structural beams, birch plywood paneling and ceilings, cherry cabinets, recycled black butt eucalyptus

Finishes

Exterior: Total Wood Protectant (TWP), Amteco 300 Series Light Cedar

Interior: Tinted stain on the fir beams (Minwax Golden Oak), clear sealer on cherry cabinets

Compass Rose

www.obiebowman.com

Exterior: Vertical redwood siding, ploughed redwood gutters

Interior: Douglas fir framing, paneling, cabinets; red ash floors

Finishes

Exterior: Cabots Weathering Stain

Interior: Clear sealer on floor, cabinets, and doors

Island Residence

www.hammerarchitects.com

Exterior: Western red cedar clapboard siding, trim, and pergola; mahogany flooring for porch and deck

Interior: Exposed Douglas fir glu-lam beams, bamboo flooring, mahogany trim

Finishes

Exterior: Clear sealer

Interior: Clear sealer

Pine Island Retreat

www.mcdonoughpartners.com

Exterior: Western red cedar siding; reclaimed western red cedar ceilings, beams, and window frames; cypress columns

Interior: Reclaimed white oak, clear-grade eastern white pine, butternut, carpathian elm, burled maple, laurel

Finishes

Exterior: WeatherTec

Interior: Livos Meldos Hard Oil finish

Maine House

www.johncolearchitect.com

Exterior: Reclaimed barn timbers for framing and exposed on the interior and porch, red cedar shingles and trim, Douglas fir

Interior: Douglas fir trim, reclaimed Douglas fir flooring and wainscot

Finishes

Exterior: Clear sealer

Interior: Clear sealer

Simon House

www.safdierabines.com

Exterior: Clear cedar

Interior: Clear cedar, cherry cabinets

Finishes

Exterior: Total Wood Protectant (TWP) tinted sealer

Interior: Tinted sealer, clear sealer for cherry cabinets

Cove House

www.somoco.com

Exterior: Reclaimed river cypress, yellow pine, driftwood, recycled redwood for exterior doors

Interior: Reclaimed river cypress for doors and some cabinets, sustainably harvested cherry for kitchen cabinets, recycled chestnut cabinets, yellow pine, oak limbs

Finishes

Exterior: No finishes used

Interior: 50/50 finish of urethane and BioShield

Villalucy

www.wpastudio.com

Exterior: Horizontal cedar boards, alder window frames

Interior: Cedar, lite ply

Finishes

Exterior: Clear sealer

Interior: Clear sealer

Weber Residence

www.obiebowman.com

Exterior: Vertical redwood siding, ploughed redwood gutters

Interior: Douglas fir ceilings, floors, and cabinets

Finishes

Exterior: No finishes used

Interior: Clear sealer on floors, cabinets, and doors

Virginia Beach House

www.mcdonoughpartners.com

Exterior: FSC-certified Spanish cedar shiplap siding, Ipe for trellis

Interior: FSC-certified cherry for flooring, grade plywood paneling, casework, reclaimed apple for benches in living room, certified southern yellow pine glu-lam beams

Finishes

Exterior: Safecoat "Polyureseal" BP satin

Interior: Clear sealer

Fallen Leaves

www.maryannthompson.com

Exterior: Horizontal western red cedar, Alaskan yellow cedar door and window trim, Alaskan yellow cedar shingles, Honduras mahogany decks and stair treads

Interior: Western red cedar soffits, beech walls in powder room, clear maple stair treads, cherry and maple cabinetry, bamboo floors

Finishes

Exterior: No finishes used

Interior: Clear sealer on floors, cabinets, and stair treads

Art Center College Library
1700 Lida St.
Pasadena, CA 91103